*The Science and Magic of Falling in Love
with Mr. or Ms. Right for You*

How to Find Your

PERFECT
PARTNER

Dr. Tina Marie Thomas & Dr. Haley Fox

How to Find Your Perfect Partner

The Science and Magic of Falling in Love with Mr. or Ms. Right for You

©2023 Dr. Tina Marie Thomas

print ISBN: 979-8-35092-666-8
ebook ISBN: 979-8-35092-667-5

Contents

Dedication

This book is dedicated to Mamie and Chief (my parents), who fell in love at first sight on February 14, 1952, and stayed in love for over sixty-five years! As I watched them adore each other through thick and thin, for better or worse, in sickness and health, my fascination with their love and "in-loveness" grew. Two crazy kids—sixty-five years of love—one fantastic love story, and the desire to help others have a chance for that kind of love are the inspiration for this book.

I will never have enough words to express the depth of my gratitude. Thank you, Mom and Dad, for living the dream of true love, which has set me on a path of trying to figure out how to help others (and myself) find the same.

Love always,
Tina Marie

Verlyn and DeForest "Jody" Corwin

…And to *my* parents, Dutch and Leone, who beat the odds by coming together from "opposite sides of the tracks" and managed to live a never-a-dull-moment marriage that lasted sixty years (and counting) and produced five remarkable children, to the bewilderment of those who thought the relationship doomed. I learned far more from your example than from your rhetoric; despite a solid German stoicism and fierce Minnesota self-sufficiency, you taught me invaluable lessons about love, family, embracing differences, and the riches that come from sticking together through thick and thin.

With Love Always,
"Helen Lee" (Haley)

Leone and Dutch Barber

Introduction
by Dr. Tina Thomas

As I begin typing this intro, I think back to a time when I was crying and heartbroken. I was so sad that it was difficult just to get through the day. I had a history of choosing amazing partners and relationships that began and ended smoothly and lovingly. Yet, I had just ended a tumultuous 18-month relationship that I should have never started. What went wrong? Oh, I know... I had not followed my own advice!

So... I feel quite qualified to write this book based on having decades of rich, healthy, and wonderful relationships and helping countless people to find excellent partners, combined with decades of counseling-challenged relationships, coupled with a humbling experience of what happened when I let my heart get ahead of my head and didn't respect the biological power of falling in love.

As therapists, Dr. Fox and I have witnessed the incredible sadness and heard the gut-wrenching stories of many brokenhearted people. Too often, the problem seems to be that they fell in love with someone who was not a good choice for them from the start. Falling in love feels like magic, and, in a way, it is. But (spoiler alert) most people don't realize that falling in love also has a rather predictable biological basis! Based on our knowledge and experience, we want to share a process that will give you better odds of falling in love with the right person for you. Then, when the "magic" happens, it will be when you want it to be, and you will have an even better chance of having a long-lasting, healthy, and happy relationship!

My impressive personal and professional track record led me to create a formula to simplify the process for people. Then, a few years ago, Dr. Fox joined me in this endeavor, and we collaborated to refine that system. We have been inspired by a new science of love by researchers like Dr. Arthur Aron and Dr. Helen Fisher. We now believe the formula and process presented in this book may revolutionize dating for anyone who genuinely seeks a well-matched partner to love.

We created this book to save you time and heartache and help you find a fantastic partner more elegantly. We hope this book will remove some mystery (and risk) from mate selection. We anticipate that it will increase your chances of finding an excellent partner who will be a better fit for you than if you randomly allowed yourself to fall in love "as fate would have it." This process has been tested with many others and with ourselves. As a result, we have witnessed people who learned how to size up potential matches and avoid what could have been a disastrous relationship. Likewise, we have seen healthier and better-suited partners find each other and establish rich and extraordinary relationships.

For Dr. Fox and myself, there is nothing quite like the feeling of helping people make their dreams come true. For many people, this includes finding a special someone with whom to share their life and dreams. We hope to add your name to a growing list of happy lovers who have found that perfect partner. Then, when you write us, it will be with tears of joy, not heartbreak!

Good luck with your search!
Tina Thomas

How to Use This Book

We designed this book to save you time and to streamline your process for finding a romantic partner who is a good fit. We based our program on some of the latest science about falling in love and mate selection. Chapter 1 is an overview of the philosophy and process that Dr. Thomas developed, and the two of us refined together. Chapter 2 lays out the premises upon which we created this book. Chapter 3 takes you through the process step-by-step. Chapter 4 is a send-off chapter alerting you to potential pitfalls along the way.

"How to Find Your Perfect Partner" is part instruction manual, part workbook, and part self-help guide, with opportunities for self-exploration and self-improvement. We suggest you read through the book at least once to get a general idea of the system and process, then use the forms in the Appendix as your workbook.

As you read, you may notice that we compare searching for a partner to a treasure hunt. This metaphor offers a vision of a kind of map as well as inspiration to take on your journey with an expectant and enthusiastic attitude. We sincerely hope the material in this book will be as valuable to you as it has been for many others, and we wish you a safe, satisfying, and successful journey!

CHAPTER ONE:

The Perfect Partner — Is that possible?

"It's a funny thing about life; if you refuse to accept anything but the best, you very often get it."

—William Somerset Maugham

The Search for Perfection

Once upon a time, a long, long time ago, a prince decided he would go on a quest to find the perfect princess. It took him ten years of searching around the world when finally, he found her! She was absolutely stunning; a brilliant, sensual, voluptuous creature, clearly every prince's dream princess in every way. When he happened upon her, he thought at first that she was a figment of his imagination. Then, he put her through rigorous testing.

She passed every test, from agility to communication skills to the womanly arts of pleasing a man.

"Oh, my goodness!" he exclaimed. "At last, I have found you. You are perfect in every way. You are The One for me. Shall we marry today or tomorrow?"

"Well," she responded, "there is one problem."

"But you are perfect!" replied the man. "What could possibly be wrong with you?"

"The problem is not with me," she replied. "The problem is with you. I am searching for the perfect prince, and you, Sir, are not The One for me."

The Perfect-for-You Partner

Before we begin, let us be clear about what a "perfect partner" is and is not. Since there is no such thing as a perfect *person*, there can technically be no such thing as a *perfect partner*. Instead, we suggest a reframe: consider the notion of a perfect partner *for you*. When we refer to your perfect partner throughout the book, we mean the person that would be perfect for YOU for now, in other words, one that fits with this particular time in your life. Of course, we are aware that people change and grow at different rates, and life-changing events happen along the way that can cause a relationship to no longer be able to serve its original purpose. We understand that the person currently perfect for you may not be so 10 or 20 years from now. Therefore, we offer no guarantee for a life-long relationship, but we are confident that this book can help you find your perfect partner *for now*. Suppose you are looking for a long–term partner and hoping for a life–long relationship. In that case, understanding and utilizing this process will significantly increase your chances of that possibility. So… who is your perfect partner? Well, only you can define that for yourself. We will guide you through an honest and clear-eyed examination and resolution of that question. Then, with a well-defined vision in mind—and after doing your emotional, physical, and spiritual "homework"—you will be much better equipped to find a mate with all the *essential* things you want and need in a relationship. If you choose the perfect partner, you will have opportunities to experience the joy, enrichment, and personal growth that good relationships bring.

The process of finding your perfect partner is a relatively simple one. We will lay out five simple basic steps in Chapter 3. Remember, "simple" is not the same as "easy." The process requires effort on your part. It also requires radical honesty with yourself and your potential partner. If you are willing to be truly honest with yourself, radically honest yet kind with others, and willing to play a game you may never have played before (which can be unsettling but promises the results you're looking for), you've come to the right place.

So… let's get started with finding your perfect partner, shall we?

CHAPTER TWO:

Why and How this System Works

To understand why and how this system works, let's begin by reviewing the seven basic premises forming our How to Find Your Perfect Partner (HTFYPP) process.

Premise #1:
FALLING IN LOVE IS A DRIVE

According to Dr. Helen Fisher,[1] a renowned expert in the biology of love, while what we call "falling in love" feels fantastic, it is actually not a feeling but a drive. It is a drive like the drive of hunger, sleep, and sex. In fact, Dr. Fisher believes that the falling-in-love drive is stronger than all the other human drives, including the sex drive. It's a pretty radical concept, eh? If you are open to the possibility that Premise #1 is possible, then you may find Premise # 2 intriguing and liberating!

Premise #2:
YOU CAN MANIPULATE DRIVES TO GET YOU WHAT YOU WANT

All drives can be manipulated to get what you want by priming or delaying the drive. For example, we can prime (or accelerate) the hunger drive by putting ourselves in a position where we can see or smell delicious food, listen to someone describe a wonderful meal, or read a recipe book and imagine how the different ingredients might taste. Alternatively, we can delay fulfilling the hunger drive simply by choosing not to turn into the first fast food restaurant we see, waiting until a specific time to eat, or even fasting. Similarly to the hunger drive, we can prime or delay the in-love drive.

Premise #3:
INTIMACY PRIMES THE IN-LOVE DRIVE AND THE "IN-LOVE DRUG"

You might be surprised to learn that the current research (and our experience) suggests that the way to prime or accelerate falling in love is to create opportunities for intimacy. Research has given us clues as to what kinds of questions and sharing create a sense of intimacy and how intimacy (along

---

1   https://helenfisher.com

with gazing into another person's eyes) speeds up the process of falling in love. (We will share more on this later in the how-to section.)

But your most valuable tool is the understanding that you can delay falling in love long enough to assess your potential partner and avoid making a drastic mistake. This is a critical piece of information because once you begin falling in love, you start a chemical cascade where your brain is quickly exposed to phenylethylamine (PEA for short), also known as the "In-Love Drug." Not only is PEA in your brain, but it is also an ingredient in chocolate, which is probably why Valentine's Day and chocolates go so well together! Phenylethylamine is an amphetamine-like drug that causes an increase in serotonin, dopamine, and norepinephrine. In the right combinations, these neurotransmitters account for that wonderfully dizzying rush of feeling associated with being in love. When a person's brain is affected by PEA, the lucky person feels bright, energetic, childlike, and happy. PEAs are very addicting and appear to be produced during the in-love state, which can last anywhere between six months to four years but can last up to seven years under certain circumstances. (Hence the seven-year itch?)

WARNING: Being in love is not like being addicted, chemically and biologically speaking; when you are in love, you are addicted to a powerful drug. (some would say it is the best drug known to humans!) Now, most people realize that addictions can lead to poor choices. So, if you have made a poor choice when you fall in love, it will be very difficult and heartbreaking to come to terms with your selection, and many complications can happen along the way. Those complications can include, but are not limited to: children, financial stressors, hurt, anger, disappointment, challenging breakups, and sadness associated with grief and loss. Do not underestimate the power of this drug!

Riding the Waves

The last time that Dr. Thomas (aka Dr. T) found herself falling in love, she noticed that she experienced cyclical waves of bright, mushy, lovely feelings. Dr. Fox was visiting her during that precious time, and Dr. T would tell her when she would get a wave of that ooey-gooey and sometimes tingly feeling usually accompanied by thoughts of her newly beloved. It seemed to occur every fifteen to twenty minutes like clockwork. The initial, almost distracting pulses lasted about three weeks. After that, there was still a very strong "high" associated with her in-love state, but it seemed that her brain had adjusted somewhat so that she could concentrate on work again, at least a little bit more. Unfortunately for Dr. T (who did not follow her advice and allowed herself to fall in love with a less-than-optimal fit), the relationship sadly and somewhat abruptly ended.

Interestingly, during the time of her breakup with her now former boyfriend, she began to feel powerful physical pangs in her gut that felt like withdrawal symptoms, which also seemed to occur every fifteen to twenty minutes for about a week. When she and her former boyfriend decided that they would be able to manage to still be friends and continue contact even though they were no longer going to be romantic partners, the physical discomfort and waves of withdrawal ceased immediately during that conversation. Hmmm... just one person's experience, but we would be interested in hearing if you also had a similar or different awareness of your body's reaction to falling in love.

Premise #4:
YOU CAN STOP YOURSELF FROM FALLING IN LOVE

It appears you can stop yourself from falling in love until a certain point. There does seem to be a biological/chemical "tipping point" or "point of no return." Once you have crossed that in-love threshold, you may find yourself "invested" (some might say shackled) in a relationship with your beloved, for better or worse, for a period of time ranging anywhere from months to years.

One of the best illustrations of the point of no return can be found in a scene from the movie *The Great Gatsby*, when the young and mysterious Jay Gatsby recounts to Nick, a journalist, the moment when he allows himself to fall in love. "I knew that when I kissed this girl, I would be forever changed. So, I stopped, and I waited. I waited for a moment longer." Nick then observed, "He knew that when he kissed this girl and forever wed his unutterable visions to her perishable breath, his mind would never romp again like the mind of God—that falling in love would change his destiny forever. Then he kissed her." At the moment of the kiss, Gatsby concludes, "Then, I just let myself go."

Watching Gatsby pause and look up to the sky before sealing his fate with a kiss crystallized a long-held suspicion of Dr. Thomas, which is that there is a moment in time in which we can consciously keep ourselves from falling in love—but once that moment has passed, if we allow the chemistry of "in-loveness" to begin, our brain lights up like a match to kerosene, (hello PEAs!) compelling us to ride out that state of in-loveness for better or worse.

So… when it comes to falling in love, we can accelerate the process, or, if we are wise, we can delay the drive (tap the PEA brakes) until we are sure we want to cross the threshold to the promised land of milk and honey of in-love land. Knowing that we have more control than we think and don't have to be a victim of ill-fitted fate is extremely useful and empowering. "Well, I know he's bad for me, but we fell in love" no longer needs to be the wedding (or divorce!) chant.

Premise #5:
CHEMISTRY IS TRICKY AND DOES NOT GUARANTEE "TRUE LOVE"

There's a reason people say they fell "madly" in love – it can be confusing and make you feel crazy. Dr. Fox will tell you that on more than one occasion, she did not choose love; but felt like love chose her. Indeed, love seemed to arrive out of nowhere. Time brings clarity, however, and with distance, the underlying factors that fed those profound experiences of "chemistry" have become easier to identify. Whenever strong chemistry comes into play, it appears to be linked to psychological needs. Often, we see admired qualities in another person that may be the same qualities we have that have not yet been adequately nurtured and are yearning to emerge. We may also project qualities of another person's unfinished business with us (perhaps from our family of origin or earlier couple relationships) to have a "corrective experience." It can get complicated fast.[2] But we do not have to give all our power to those emotional responses. Instead, we can learn what drives us unconsciously so that our choices are better informed.

You have more control over who you fall in love with than some romantic novels would have you believe. By adopting clear criteria in your conscious mind and by doing the necessary homework to prepare mentally, emotionally, physically, and spiritually for the relationship you desire, you elevate your well-being, making it more likely that you will attract a healthier partner and have a much better chance of having a healthy and satisfying relationship as a result.

This process requires using your head rather than solely relying upon your heart (or hormones!) to guide you. Falling in love has been compared with insanity; at the very least, it tends to blind us to certain realities. Under the influence of PEAs, specific habits or predispositions in our new partner may initially seem charming. Still, later, without the chemical "in-love" lubrication, those same behaviors may drive you mad. Choose wisely!

Premise #6:
THERE ARE MANY "MR RIGHTS" AND "MS RIGHTS"

That's right. We don't believe in a one-and-only Mr. Right or Ms. Right. While we believe in soulful connections, we don't think you necessarily have a one-and-only "soulmate."

---

2   For a more detailed explanation of how these love themes are created and subconsciously perpetuated you can read "Getting the Love You Want" by Harville Hendricks

It is essential to recognize that human beings, as potential partners, may be more interchangeable than we have previously believed. We all know of marriages that ended in death or divorce, in which partners became happily re-married or otherwise partnered with different significant others. Some—including those who have themselves experienced divorce—may have jumped to the conclusion that their earlier marriages were "mistakes" or "failures," simply because they did not last. Such chastisement may be entirely misplaced. It is more likely that you may have chosen the perfect partner for you at that time and outgrew that phase or that you chose a partner who was a link to some unfinished emotional business lurking in your unconscious memory banks that needed to be resolved. Either way, a little compassion and forgiveness for you and your former partner for being human goes a long way and frees you up to be more available and healthier in your next relationship.

Spoiler alert…ultimately, The One may actually be yourself! To understand this idea, the song, The One (https://soundcloud.com/user-113677170) (Fox, 2000) describes a series of important relationships, each representing a search for The One that ended in disappointment. Dr. Fox's tendency to frame her romantic quest this way changed when she realized one day, long after this song was written, that she was The One, the real object of her quest. She did not need another person to "complete" her. That realization enabled a reframing of her desire for a genuinely equal partner who could share and celebrate their mutual "at-oneness."

Premise #7:
IF YOUR "RAS" IS IN GEAR THEN YOUR PATH WILL BE CLEAR

Have you ever noticed that when you get something new – a new car, outfit, cell phone, etc.- it suddenly seems like you spot that new thing everywhere you go? That phenomenon can last a few days or weeks, depending on how excited you are about your "new thing." Over time, your brain adjusts, and the excitement and awareness of other things that are similar to your "new thing" gradually fade away. We think this phenomenon happens because of activating a filter in your brain known as the reticular activating system.

The RAS, a shorthand term for the reticular activating system, is the filter in your brain that, when energized with emotion and vivid images, especially in life-threatening situations, helps increase the odds of survival. It also helps you to recruit resources quickly to achieve your goals.[3] When a person is emotionally energized by a goal, the RAS enables you to see opportunities for achieving that goal that may not have been as apparent when the RAS had not been activated. To enhance your search for a romantic partner, you can activate the RAS to help you speed up this process and get even more elegant and dynamic results.

One of Dr. T's favorite examples of how the RAS works (that came from life experience – don't ask!) involves imagining you walking alone in the desert. You may at first enjoy looking at puffy clouds and the many shapes they take, or you might enjoy watching birds flying overhead and daydreaming about what it might be like to soar like a bird. But as you gradually run out of water and fear that without water, you might die, strong emotional responses trigger the RAS to engage. No longer are fluffy clouds and birds a source of amusement or entertainment; instead, you look to them for clues to survival. You begin to look at the clouds, hoping for rain, or notice the flight paths of birds overhead ("Are they flying to water or away from water?") to discern possible water sources. Your sharpened focus increases your odds of sooner rather than later results.

When you apply this understanding to life in general, you will notice that your RAS is activated when you experience vivid images of what you want and do not want. You will begin to see and hear opportunities for meeting other people. In addition, when the RAS is activated, not only does it sharpen our senses and help us find what we are looking for, but it also increases our goal attainment efficiency. It helps save time by keeping us

---

3   For a more detailed explanation of getting your RAS in gear, see Dr. Tina Thomas's book, *The Ultimate Edge – How to Be, Do, and Get Anything You Want.*

focused on things related to achieving our goals and keeps us from wasting our time on things that don't help us reach our goals. The activation will also heighten your awareness of potential partners in your immediate surroundings. You will likely spend less time looking for love "in all the wrong places."

Getting your RAS in gear and being clear about what you want and don't want is incredibly important and will give you the energy and focus to find your treasured love.

So there…Now that you understand our basic premises, are you ready to take the steps to find your perfect partner? If the answer is "yes" then read on!

CHAPTER THREE:

Creating and Navigating Your Map

ACTION PLAN

A man who stands on hill with his mouth open
will wait a long time for roast duck to drop in.

~ Confucius

Anything worthwhile will require some effort, and finding your
perfect partner is no exception.

Finding your future partner is like going on an adventure to find hidden
treasure. Clearly, a treasure hunt as crucial as this one requires careful preparation. This step is where the rubber meets the road. We suggest you do the
five steps in this chapter one at a time and in order, at least initially. Once

you have completed all the steps, you can return to earlier steps to fine-tune them, but you risk not getting the desired results if you skip them.

STEP ONE:
Define the Treasure

You cannot begin to pursue your destination without first being clear about what that destination is. Therefore, before starting a treasure hunt, you must clearly know what "treasure" you seek. To ward against ultimate disappointment, you must begin by making a "non-negotiables" list of your future partner's traits and characteristics. That list needs to include everything that you absolutely *must have* and everything that you absolutely *do not want* to have in a romantic partner. For starters, we suggest that you have no fewer than ten and no more than thirty non-negotiable items.

Just a note here that everybody has a list! If you think you don't, it is simply because you are unaware of it. For anyone who says they don't have a list, all you have to do to disprove that is to ask them if they are okay with a smoker or non-smoker, or someone 30 years younger or older, or someone who has a history of being dishonest, etc. Most people who were not initially aware of having some criteria will have emphatic and clear responses to their unconscious list!

We recommend starting by brainstorming or creating a collage on a large sheet of paper. (Appendix A) Begin by writing down every essential quality and trait or cut out pictures of those attributes. Rigorous honesty is critical here. Include every item you can think of without censoring anything. Later, you can prune the list based on your best judgment and thoughtful recollection. At that point, after careful review, you can list your core non-negotiables. (Appendix B) We provided Dr. Thomas' list in Appendix C for an example of a non-negotiables list.

While determining your non-negotiables, it may help to examine your past relationships and ask yourself which qualities worked well for you and which traits or circumstances eroded your happiness. Each can give you clues about the most important things you truly desire or require in an ideal partner at this time in your life. Also, please be clear about what type of relationship you seek. (Appendix D) Are you looking for casual dating, marriage, a hangout partner, or an intimate, long-term relationship? Your non-negotiables for a hangout partner may differ significantly from those for a husband or mother of your children.

Remember that your initial judgment may not always produce a list that genuinely points towards the sort of relationship that can support your mental, emotional, physical, and spiritual health. Most of us allow ourselves to be influenced to some degree by what the people who love us want *for* us, sometimes without knowing us as well as we know ourselves. We may contribute to this phenomenon by hiding or feeling shy about revealing our true desires to others. Many of us carry distorted notions of what we *ought* to want. This distortion is especially prevalent in areas of attitudes related to religion/spirituality, money, and sex. Desiring a partner who is more or less religious, more or less wealthy, or to whom sex is more or less important may feel embarrassing to admit. However, a lack of clarity in acknowledging or sharing those desires can confuse you and your potential partner when determining a fit. Take care to be kind to yourself but also honest with yourself. Remember there is no such thing as a good or bad, right or wrong non-negotiable – only more accurate or less clear descriptions that match your needs and desires.

A Kiss is Just a Kiss, but a Nonnegotiable is Not Just a Nonnegotiable

Anne, a 48-year-old fitness instructor and personal trainer, struggled with one of her non-negotiables - "a man who is physically fit with a few extra pounds being okay." But Anne wondered if it was shallow to consider body weight a non-negotiable item. Even though health and activity were a considerable part of her life, she didn't want to appear "superficial" and "all about looks." So, when Anne met Paul, she was torn.

He was tall, handsome, intelligent, and had a great sense of humor, but Paul was about 50 pounds overweight. Because he was so incredible in every other way, she decided to waive that one non-negotiable and got involved with him; after all, as a fitness instructor, she figured she could help him lose weight. Anne didn't want to seem elitist or judgmental about body weight, so she waived that criterion. But much to her surprise and disappointment, she began to gain weight by picking up some of Paul's bad habits!

Binge-watching TV, overindulging in desserts, and shirking workouts became crystalized patterns in their relationship. Over time, she also realized that Paul's weight was a symptom of a lifetime history of untreated depression. When she would go out of town for a week, she would come home to a refrigerator full of poor choices and see that Paul had gained a few extra pounds. To make matters worse, he also left lots of nasty cigar stubs in the bottom of the trash can. Over time, she began to resent Paul's lack of regard for her need for a healthier lifestyle. It wasn't until a hiking trip during which Paul constantly held up the expedition to catch his breath and left Anne responsible for gathering firewood (since he was too tired to help) that she realized the issue could not be ignored. This mismatch in lifestyle was making her feel like she was aging prematurely and was creating too much tension and unhappiness. Anne eventually ended the relationship because it was too unhealthy for her. As Anne discussed the breakup with us, she was quite sad, but she realized that for her, physical health reflected mental health and that someone who was more than a few pounds overweight was, in fact, not a good fit for her. She also learned that denying the importance of that nonnegotiable eventually undermined the entire relationship. Looking at weight as a non-negotiable without judging it as superficial or right or wrong simplified the process of finding her next partner. A few months after her breakup with Paul, Anne excitedly reported that her new beau, Raymond, was not only health-conscious; he also inspired her to adopt a more plant-based diet and to do couples yoga before bed, both practices that added value to her life. Rather than struggling to pull someone along to her way of living, Anne's new partner helped her become an even healthier version of her already healthy self! She and Raymond are living happily ever after, working towards opening a boutique health club and fitness center.

After you feel clear about the ten to thirty qualities or traits that comprise your non-negotiables, you may also want to prepare a second list of features that would be *nice* to have but are not "deal-breakers." These can be considered "icing on the cake" or "bonus points" for things you like that are not deal-breakers. For instance, having a partner who likes to cook and appreciates fine wine might be nice, but these features may not be essential. Ask yourself: If your potential partner scored 100% on your must-have/must-not-have non-negotiables, would you check them off the list because of this missing item? If the answer is "no," it's a bonus. Bonus points come in handy when trying to get clarity in non-negotiables. Sometimes, as you may discover in your journey, you may get the two confused. No worries – just keep notes on your awareness as you refine your needs versus preferences. Once you have a list of non-negotiables and bonus points, you will have a much better idea of what your perfect partner "looks like," and you will be more likely to recognize them when they appear before you. And sometimes, with experience, you may find that bonus points are non-negotiables and vice versa.

Suggested questions to help you discover your
non-negotiables:

- What values are important to you?

- What traits can you not tolerate in a person?

- What do you need in a relationship to feel satisfied?

- What are your "deal-breakers"?

- Is age important?

- Appearance?

- Education?

- Temperament?

- Introversion/extroversion?

- Alcohol and drug use?

- Smoking versus non-smoking?

- Willingness to engage in public displays of affection?

- Sexual appetite?

- Sexual preferences?

- Financial situation?

- Goals and dreams?

- Hobbies?

- Level of activity?

- How much private/alone time is required?

- Special issue/idiosyncrasies/concerns?

- Monogamy versus open or polyamorous relationships?

- Children? How many? When?

STEP TWO:
Be the Partner You Want to Attract

Another challenge in determining non-negotiables arises when we require potential love interests to fill real or imagined deficits in us. Our initial unexamined criteria may conceal the problematic belief that we depend on another person to "complete us" by compensating for unfinished self-work. This step requires you to review the list of non-negotiable items you prepared. It is time now to "check it twice." This is the time to take the opportunity to evaluate whether *you* embody those qualities.

As you determine how many features you possess on your list, check these off one at a time and be brutally honest. It never hurts to "check your math" with a trusted friend. If one of the traits you would like in your perfect partner is to "have a sense of humor," ask yourself, "Do *I* have a sense of humor?" Then ask a friend if they agree. Do this for all your items. By the same token, when doing your inventory, you need to be sure that you are fair in appraising your strengths. We don't want you selling yourself short and asking for far less in a partner than you expect of yourself.

After careful review of whether (or not) YOU would meet your own requirements for a partner, we suggest that if you meet fewer than, say, 80% of your list, you consider taking some time to either amend your criteria, or better yet, to work on yourself before seeking a new relationship. If you don't do your personal "homework" you may be limiting yourself to a less optimal mate and relationship. "Water seeks its own level," as they say, and it may be advantageous to wait until you are at a higher level of functioning so that you may acquire those qualities you value in a partner. The good news is experience has taught us that those qualities people truly desire in another tend to be qualities just below the surface within ourselves. Therefore, taking time to cultivate what you have not yet developed could work in your favor in the long run.

If you find one or more non-negotiables in which you are not even in the same ballpark as what you require in a potential partner, you must stop right here and right now. Why? Well, let's take the sense of humor as an example. If you seek a partner with a good sense of humor, but you are personally less fun than watching paint dry, then it is unlikely a person with a good sense of humor would enjoy being with *you!*

Consider people you know personally who set themselves up for frustration. For example, I recall a friend of a friend who always sought stunning "super-model" women, while he himself was unattractive by cultural standards. (I can't tell you how many times I have worked with older, obviously out-of-shape men who tell me that they are looking for a "fine, sexy, younger woman." I must stop them at that point and, as gently as possible, ask them, "Dude, have you looked at yourself since high school?!?" And then lovingly suggest that either they need to lower their standards a bit or hit the gym!) Or perhaps you can think of someone who is always attracted to highly educated people to compensate for their lack of confidence in their own intelligence? Beware of entirely opposite requirements, such as a destitute person seeking a financial "savior." Extreme opposite requirements are a red flag signaling an actual or perceived deficit and are usually a recipe for frustration and disappointment. If, by some chance, you find you would honestly rate yourself with a big fat "zero" in *any* of your categories, STOP! Dare to ask yourself whether you are upholding a double standard. Is it okay for you to fall short but not your partner?

So, let's pause and review: If you discover a non-negotiable that doesn't reflect your current attributes, you have two options: remove that pesky feature from your list and refrain from complaining if your partner lacks that quality, or cultivate that trait in yourself first. Once you align with your list, that is, once you have verified that you are everything you are asking for, you can be more confident in your search as you move to step three.

STEP THREE:
Prepare Yourself with the Right Attitude

Quick Test: Develop an "ATM Mentality."

How do you respond if you put a dollar bill into a dollar bill changer or an ATM, and it spits back your dollar bill?

a. Collapse into a crying heap - take it personally and vow never to be rejected again.

b. Keep trying to put the same dollar bill in different ways, over and over, hoping to make it work.

c. Try a different dollar bill, and if you are not successful, keep trying different bills until you find one that fits

If you chose "a" or "b" in the ATM Mentality Quiz, it's time to see a therapist or life coach first! If you selected "c," you may read on.

Develop an ATM Mentality.

ATM stands for A Tough Mental Attitude. In the context of our program, ATM means learning how to not take "rejection" (i.e., not a good fit) personally by developing the insight, discipline, and grace to move on. Remember, a dollar bill changer has specific criteria – it has a template for rejection and acceptance – it requires a particular color green, at least three corners, the head in a specific direction, etc. Even if your dollar bill does not meet the machine's criteria, it doesn't mean it is inferior. It's still worth 100 cents! Likewise, when you don't fit someone else's non-negotiable list, it doesn't mean you have less value – it simply means you are not the fit they are looking for.

Turn "failure" into "feedback."

The first part of this step requires that you begin this preparation so that no matter what you do, *you cannot lose*. From this moment forward, please strike the word "failure" from your vocabulary and replace it with the word "feedback."

A failure mindset will discourage you and make you feel like you did something wrong. A feedback mindset interprets any "speedbumps" or missteps as an opportunity for learning and mastery. For example, let's say one of your non-negotiables is "must be addiction-free," and on the very first date, the person across from you drinks heavily. You know within an hour that your date is an active alcoholic, and the best thing for both of you is to end the date before dessert. But…after the fifth or sixth "wish you could've been there when we got crazy drunk" story, your date suggests you go out dancing after dinner. Perhaps you agree to this suggestion to spare your date's feelings despite knowing this is a dead-end date. After an hour or two of watching your date get more drunk than a sailor on Saturday night, it is easy to beat yourself up about not being precise or socially adept enough to put an end to a date going from bad to worse. However, we suggest you reframe your experience as an opportunity to learn how to extricate yourself from a dead-end date in the future. Maybe your desire to be "nice" interferes with your need to be forthright about your time and relationship needs. Or perhaps you will find the solution is to create shorter, time-limited dates for coffee that are easier to end if things are not going well. Incidentally, learning to end dates gracefully saves time and builds confidence in nipping suboptimal relationships in the bud. Practice makes possible!

Thinking "Feedback" rather than "Failure" also needs to continue through the remaining steps. Once you adopt this mindset related to dating, you might want to apply this attitude to all areas of your life. When it comes to mindsets, it's a keeper!

Increase your numbers for better a better outcome.

If you recall Premise #6: "There are many 'Mr. Rights' and 'Ms. Rights' since as human beings, we are biologically interchangeable". This philosophy means we are like puzzle pieces. Some pieces fit better than others. Some don't fit at all. And a few fit close to perfectly. It is easier to find a good fit when you have a large selection of high-quality choices to choose from. In other words, finding a perfect partner for now is a numbers game. So, having a large pool of choices means you need to plan on misses, soon and often, and preparing for that inevitable outcome will help you get through to your perfect partner with minimal emotional wear and tear.

If you want to say "Hello" to a new relationship, make sure you have said "Goodbye" to the old one(s).[4]

It is also vital that you check yourself and your intentions. Once you are clear about what you are looking for in a partner, it's time to clear a space for your partner to arrive. Sometimes, that means clearing away psychological clutter and debris from old relationships, including haunting memories of people who may be taking up premium real estate in your life and consciousness. First and foremost, you must be emotionally available to ensure the odds are stacked in your favor. If you want to be able to say "hello" to a new relationship in a healthy way, regardless of how your past relationship(s) ended, it is critical to honestly say "goodbye" to the hurts, regrets, and disappointments of past relationships.

Correct self-sabotaging and couple-destruct recurrent themes.

Do you feel as though you have experienced a pattern of attracting the "wrong person" time and time again? If so, you may want to consider that the pattern is likely to continue until you get to the bottom of it and do some course corrections. Consider the beliefs, situations, habits, or behavioral styles that could unconsciously sabotage a future relationship. A good indicator is examining beliefs, conditions, and behaviors that have a recurring theme that has

---

4 If you have a hard time saying "good-bye" you might benefit from Dr. Thomas' fourth book, "The G-Word". She offers a couple of novel ways to say good-bye and feel better on the other side.

sabotaged your *past* relationships.[5] You may have noticed that even though the names have changed, the themes remain the same. For instance, Carol came to her first session complaining that every man she had been seriously involved with just didn't "get her." Our discussion revealed that Carol's parents were both working professionals who put their career needs before their children's emotional and mental needs and often left the children fending for themselves to fulfill those needs. To add insult to injury, when her parents had to work in the evening, Carol and her brother's inexperienced babysitters spent more time talking on the phone than to the children. So, when Carol ventured out into the adult world, she was unconsciously attracted to high-powered professional men who often spent half of their date night on the phone texting or stepping out to take important calls. While these patterns were unpleasant, they were hauntingly familiar. Until she reviewed those unconscious patterns and the self-sabotaging beliefs that went with those patterns, she was doomed to repeat patterns learned in childhood.

Therefore, it is essential to examine your beliefs about love and your self-worth and reprogram any beliefs that do not support attracting and keeping a healthy partner (e.g., "I'm not attractive enough"; "I don't make enough money"; "All the good ones are taken"). As noted, your unconscious mind can make your beliefs seem true. It reminds us of Henry Ford's wise words: "Whether you think you can, or you think you can't – you're right."

If a belief does not support what you want, it is time to drop it and develop beliefs that do. This phenomenon includes that your unconscious mind responds to your *feelings* about yourself; if you feel unworthy or undeserving, your life experiences will reflect that.

---

5   Dr. Thomas has worked intensively for decades helping people to understand how to rewire their self-sabotaging imprints where themes stay the same and only the names in your life change. Her book, The Ultimate Edge is a must read for quick and dynamic instruction on reprogramming themes that need healthier and happier endings!

Fall in love with yourself.

You can't expect someone else to fall in love with you if you do not love yourself. When we judge or criticize ourselves, we push others away. Self-criticism utterly repels potential mates. On the other hand, self-love is highly attractive; in fact, it can be irresistible. (To be clear, we are not talking about a selfish narcissistic obsession with oneself – but simply good old-fashioned high regard and respect for oneself.)

HOW TO FALL IN LOVE WITH YOURSELF:

Make a list of ten characteristics you genuinely love about your-self, and put this list where you can see it every day. It doesn't matter what is on the list as long as it easily generates good feelings toward yourself. The more you focus on what you love about yourself, the more self-love you will experience. Others will fall in love with you, too, simply because it feels great to be around people who love themselves.

Enjoy yourself now.

Don't wait for love to find you to start living. You will attract what you are: If you are a couch potato, you will attract a couch potato. If you desire an active mate who goes skiing and is interesting, you had better start jogging, hitting the slopes, and hanging out at a bookstore or self-improvement seminar. Don't wait for them to arrive to live your best life. Start living your best life right now.

Think of yourself now and think of yourself in your perfect relation-ship. How are you different? Who do you become in the relationship? If, for example, your answer is, "I become more relaxed, confident, loving, and kind."; your answer is your clue to who you must become or return to *now*.

Embrace Jealousy.

In Dr. Thomas's book, *The Ultimate Edge*, she describes the positive inten-tions of what we typically consider "negative" emotions. One of those very misunderstood emotions is jealousy. It is natural to feel jealous when someone already has what we desire. But what if jealousy were an indicator of what we are *about to become, do, or have?* Instead of knocking or criticizing the object of our jealousy, we might consider cultivating those traits. For instance, if we feel jealous of people in healthy and happy relationships, instead of wishing disaster upon them, try identifying the relationship elements we desire for ourselves. By paying attention to precisely what we are jealous of (the playful nature of another couple, ability to communicate or accomplish goals together, etc.), we are more likely to attract and experience those positive aspects of the relationship.

STEP FOUR:
The Search

Once you have completed the first three steps, it is time to go on your Treasure Hunt. Success here depends on exposure and requires meeting as many new people as possible. You must place yourself in situations where you feel at home (enough) to attract the kind of person you want. For example, if you are an athlete or identify as a health nut, going to juice bars may make more sense than going to wine bars. Letting others know what you are looking for is a good idea, too. Some clients have offered "finder's fees" to friends and family members to help them understand how important this search is and that a little help would be greatly appreciated!

The more time you spend on your quest, the sooner you will find what you're looking for, but as human beings, we can find all sorts of reasons to hesitate here. We can delay our search indefinitely due to "not feeling ready," dreading the dating process, fear of rejection, or anything else our fear of the unknown causes us to think. No matter what the "reason" (or excuse?) may be, please remember a slogan that originated from Silicon Valley to encourage entrepreneurs to move forward in making their business dreams come true: "Fail fast – fail often." The logic behind that saying is that the more you make and learn from mistakes, the faster you will find what you want. Since we don't identify with the word "failure," perhaps it makes more sense to say, "Feedback fast – Feedback often." In other words, don't be afraid to meet as many people as possible. Then, as soon as you realize they are not a good fit, let them go, make appropriate adjustments, and keep moving forward. Wasting your time and energy because you are lonely, bored, or hoping to give it a little more time so that this person might work out is one of the biggest mistakes rookies make in this area. (Just for the record, even pros like us have succumbed!) If you find yourself temporarily "stuck" in a pre-relationship pattern that does not feel like a good fit, please be easy on yourself. Just do what it takes to let go and move on to make yourself available for the perfect partner who might be right around the corner. Remember, you are also doing the other person a favor by releasing them to continue their quest.

This is also an excellent time to reflect on expanding your life horizons. Consider being open not just to places and people who share your current interests but maybe throw in a few potential new interests and curiosities. (Pickleball, anyone?) Openness to experiencing life with people whose ideas and lifestyles reflect different values about fun, food, health, children, relationships, and love can lead to enriching new experiences. Orienting ourselves this way enables personal growth, and with this change, it may be necessary to tweak our non-negotiable criteria.

If you are getting sufficient exposure after a couple of months but not getting the desired results, consider how your non-negotiables may limit potential growth and whether any need refinement. (But don't settle!) For example, Susan, a 58-year-old retired schoolteacher, recently ended a relationship because her previous partner's two unemployed adult children absorbed most of his time and financial resources. At this stage in her life, Susan's hampered desire for travel and adventure led to stress and resent-ment. As a result, one of her non-negotiables read, "Partner must not have children under 18 or living at home." Searching for her perfect partner, Susan almost wrote off an extraordinary man as a possible partner because he had a 15-year-old daughter. However, upon further investigation, she discovered his ex-wife was the daughter's primary caretaker, and the girl was already mature enough to live overseas for short periods for college preparation. Through this process, Susan realized it was not the child's actual age that was non-negotiable but her partner's mental, emotional, and physical availability to experience life with her that truly mattered. She simply revised her non-negotiable to "Partner must not have children under 18 living at home." And at that point, she got exactly what she was looking for!

Intimacy – The Key to Falling in Love

Remember Premise #3- Intimacy primes the "In-love Drive" and the "In-Love Drug"? We cannot overstate the importance of having intimate conversations on topics that matter to you. We highly recommend Gillian Jacobs' popular blog, "To Fall in Love, Do This," which presents thirty-six love-inducing questions. Jacobs believes, like many in the field of research on love and falling in love, that taking the time to have conversations about these particularly intimate questions will inevitably lead to keen feelings of tenderness and love. [6]

By revealing vulnerable aspects of our personality, intimate questions elicit strong emotional responses in ways that ordinary conversations do not. Many social biologists believe intimacy coupled with at least four minutes of eye-gazing initiates the chemical cascade of falling in love. Hint: with this knowledge, you will never look at romantic movies the same way. But don't take our word for it - pay attention to the next romantic film and look for the moment when they express a deep personal truth at a cozy niche coffee shop, for instance. It's an intimate moment. The listening other may wipe away a tender tear and then (wait for it…) In the next scene, our lovebirds are romping in a park together, riding bikes, or throwing snowballs at each other like children. (Helloooo PEA's!)

So, if intimacy is the key to releasing in-love bliss, let's ensure you know what intimacy is. Anne Teachworth, founder of the New Orleans Gestalt Institute, described intimacy as being "into ME…see?" (Cute, eh?) Intimacy is a sense of deep heart-to-heart connection. Therefore, intimate

---

6   Gillian Jacobs' popular blog, "To Fall in Love, Do This" follow this link: https://www. nytimes.com/2015/01/11/fashion/no-37-big-wedding-or-small.html?_r=0.

conversations are generally not about intellectual concepts like the weather or current events. Intimate conversations reveal who you are, your core values, and what personal events have affected you in important ways.

Learning to initiate and engage another human being in intimate conversation is critical for connecting with another human being. Don't hesitate to lay your mental, emotional, physical, and spiritual cards on the table when getting to know someone. But timing and pacing are essential here. You don't want to overload your date with too much information all at once! Frank conversations with your potential partner can be tricky at first. Keep in mind that it's a bit like volleyball. Throw a bit of self-revealing information across the net, wait for some sharing of near-equal weight or degree of intimacy, and repeat at a leisurely pace.

When your potential partner shares their intimate moments, you will observe non-negotiables rise to the surface, which can help you determine your desired fit. Be careful here and try not to appear as if you are trying to uncover their potential shortcomings. In other words, do your best to keep the conversation flowing in a "human-friendly" and relaxed way. Remember that being a good listener is essential to evaluating your compatibility with someone. Some tactfulness is required to engage your partner with questions about what they desire or wish to avoid without "interviewing" them. It will help to review some intimate "starter questions" that you feel comfortable asking and maybe even practice asking them so you can weave them into your conversation and not feel or appear awkward. (You will find examples in the sidebar too.) If you feel bold enough, you can directly say, "I am beginning to like you, but I am reluctant to get more involved without knowing some critical information. I know these questions might normally be reserved for later, but I'm curious to see if our core values are at least a match. Let's not waste each other's time and risk bruised hearts on either side."

Suggested questions to ask your potential partner:

- "What do you seek in a partnership? What are you unwilling to bend on?"

- "How is it that you are single now?"

- "If you could re-live your life, would you do anything differently?"

- "What is the most valuable lesson you learned from your previous love relationships?"

- "What do you think your previous partner might say was the most challenging thing about living with you?"

- "Where do you see yourself in five years?"

- "What's on your bucket list?"

- "I am really beginning to like you, but I am reluctant to get more involved with you without knowing some critical information...." (Share your non-negotiables.)

Intimacy involves being willing to risk and disclose vulnerabilities to the other for connection. Since intimacy involves sharing things close to your heart, this can make you feel vulnerable, which can feel uncomfortable and even a little scary. The perceived risk is usually a concern that if you share something personal about yourself and the other person is offended or uncomfortable with your sharing, they may not like you or want to be with you anymore. That way of thinking begs the question: "Why would we want to be with someone who is not loving us and able to accept us as we truly are in the first place?".

Exposing our inner selves, beliefs, values, dreams, and tender feelings takes courage and trust in ourselves and our worth. It's also helpful to understand that the discomfort of being vulnerable may not just be a psychological challenge. Discomfort with vulnerability also has a biological underpinning that can be observed and overridden. The biological component happens because all sentient creatures instinctively know survival involves protecting their vulnerability. Examples of protecting vulnerability in natural settings include a deer trying to keep a lion away from its soft underbelly or a squid squirting ink to avoid being lunch for a hungry shark. Being seen and sharing our "soft spots," our frailty, our imperfect "humanness" may illicit the same physical discomfort as a zebra might feel alone in the plains without tall grasses to hide behind. This may be the underpinning of most humans' fear of public speaking (being "exposed" and therefore vulnerable to "attack," even if only figuratively.) If you are aware of some hesitancy to share something revealing about yourself, please assess the safety of your situation. Suppose the person you wish to be more connected with has earned your trust by holding you gently in their heart with previous personal information and has demonstrated kindness and generosity of spirit with you, themselves, and others in situations where mistakes were made, or human fragility was experienced. In that case, sharing personal information will create a heart-to-heart and tender connection nine out of ten times. If this does not happen and you experience rejection – you can confidently say goodbye to someone who cannot accept you unconditionally.

Paying Attention to Content, Process, and the Narrative

To become savvy in the selection process, it helps to pay attention to the content (what someone talks about) and the process (how someone talks about something). Observing the content and process when someone is talking will reveal how a person sees themselves and others; it helps you determine how you might eventually fit into their life narrative (or not).

If the person across from you on your date talks about their former partner in a disrespectful way versus a generous manner - get ready to throw some flags! Consider the difference between: "My ex was a total lying, worthless, cheating, basket case, so and so" and "My former partner had some mental and emotional challenges, and sadly, we outgrew each other." Either sentence could describe the same scenario but in two very different ways. The content and process of what and how your date describes someone else may reveal more about your date than the person they are describing! Using respectful words when describing another person's shortcomings indicates maturity and generosity of spirit. Harsh and disrespectful words indicate immaturity and often suggest that there is still some unfinished business or closure – like taking responsibility, granting forgiveness, or saying "good-bye." Speaking of saying "good-bye," how your date expresses their emotions is also significant. Suppose your potential partner still has an emotional "charge" (obvious anger, sadness, or hurt) when describing their history. In that case, it may indicate that they may not be complete with their past relationship issues and may not be as emotionally available and ready for a relationship as you might be.

Psst...Your Projection is Showing

Part of a person's narrative can include the process of projection, which involves projecting one's thoughts and attitudes onto others. It's a very common phenomenon and can be helpful when it comes to empathy and compassion for other human beings. Projection is an assumption about how we might feel (or have felt) in similar circumstances. For instance, seeing someone becoming tearful when talking about a former partner might remind us of when we felt sad in a similar circumstance. It will evoke tender feelings toward them as we assume they miss their partner. So, it is important to verify others' feelings since we might not have enough information to be accurate with our assumption. For example, their tears may be related to guilt, embarrassment, or missing their pet that went with their former partner!

It can also be tricky (and very revealing) when we don't realize that some of our projections are simply unknown aspects of ourselves. I learned this when I was in a brief relationship with a psychologist. I shall always be grateful to him for teaching me what I call a "cheap therapist trick." Here's what happened: one day, after a bike riding date while in a coffee shop, he said, "So Tina, we've been seeing each other for about three weeks now, and it seems like you are still interested in getting to know me. I'm curious if you could tell me what you like most about me now in our friendship?" I responded, "Oh, that's easy! You are smart, funny, and have a lot of integrity. I also like that you are non-judgmental, interested in helping others to be healthier, and seem very balanced mentally, emotionally, physically, and spiritually!" I smiled, happy with my ability to quickly target traits in him that were meaningful to me. He smiled back, almost smugly, and said, "Well, thanks for telling me a little bit more about you!" What?!? ahhh... and then the lightbulb went off! All those things I admired about him were traits I had cultivated and appreciated about myself! Positive self-projection!

An exciting twist on this question happened many years later when I was smitten with a handsome and charming man. When I asked him, "What do you like most about me so far?" he lit up and said, "Oh, that's easy! I like how you like me!" "Hmmm," I thought, "That's not really about me, so let me pay attention before getting more emotionally involved." And sure enough, within a couple more weeks, I discovered that my potential partner was quite a narcissist! Whew! Although he appeared to be quite a catch, his self-absorption was too high of a price of admission, so I opted out of moving forward with him.

Over time, I noticed that people can (and often do) project their feelings on inanimate objects and conditions. For instance, a rainy day can be described by someone who is depressed as "dark and gloomy," while someone who is content might describe the same weather as "cozy and peaceful." Pay attention!

A side note for mental health and peace of mind: From observing the process of projection repeatedly, I came to understand that when other people judged me, especially with feedback that seemed emotionally charged, I did not have to take their comments personally. When someone criticizes me, and it feels harsh or unfair, I now understand that their words might have more to do with them (or their history) than mine. Therefore, I can observe them compassionately and not feel hurt by their words.

Suppose there is a question about whether someone's feedback is valuable information or simply a hurtful projection. In that case, it helps to pay attention to the direction and amount of criticism the person in question shares. So, for example, if someone is complaining that 90% of her cell phone calls are difficult to hear, and you notice that she is the only one in your phone circle that you often don't hear well, then it is safe to assume that her cell phone is likely defective. Using the "cell phone concept" while listening to other people's stories, pay attention to the percentage of kind and complimentary versus harsh and judgmental descriptors a person uses when describing past relationships, former lovers, friends, and people at work. If they appear to have difficulty with most people, perhaps it's not simply a case of *others* being difficult.

One last piece of information on projection that you may find helpful relates to this sage advice, "Tell the truth – not so that others will believe you, but so that you can believe others." In other words, you will project trust onto others if you are trustworthy. If you are a not-so-trustworthy person, you will be suspicious of others and unable to trust them easily because you project the assumption that others, like you, must have some hidden agenda. Likewise, be careful if you are trustworthy (open, honest, and direct) since you may be biased to take another person's word because you are projecting your tendency to be transparent in sharing with others. The cautionary note here is to pay attention to your date's actions over a period of time rather than simply taking them at their word. This understanding of projection is valuable for mate selection and can be applied to dealing with all human beings in all areas of life!

"SAPPING" Your Way to a Perfect Partner for You

Finding a good fit partner takes some time (and practice). You will probably not find your perfect partner immediately. Lightning strikes are rare. So, you may want to consider the process of pursuing "sequential approximations" (SAPs) to find your perfect partner. Using sequential approximation is an incremental process of achieving one's goals in sequence and getting closer and closer (approximating) to the goal you seek as you continue to move forward. The simplest example of this is the children's game Marco Polo. In

Marco Polo, a wandering blindfolded child trying to tag others is guided by the call and response of those in pursuit. By calling out the distance in terms of temperature, such as "warmer, warmer, cooler, warmer, hotter, really hot, the blindfolded child localizes their target. Likewise, we can use our dating experiences to test whether the people who fit our criteria are right for us or if our non-negotiables need refinement. By this method, we expect the fifth or sixth partner to align more with our tastes than the first or second. For example, if you frequent local bars with no luck, you may try a gym or health club where the average patron will likely be in better mental and physical shape. Then, if still not successful, maybe your next step could be to seek family-friendly clubs offering stress management or yoga sessions that attract clientele with a holistic orientation better suited to your preferences. Using the framework of "sapping" your way to success helps with patience and appreciating the minor victories and progress along the way.

Cutting Your Losses – Save Time and Heartache

By allowing ourselves to be seen, we "put ourselves on the line," knowing that the reactions of others to our sharing are out of our control. However, if you don't take those risks early on, you and your potential partner will only discover these intimate truths after you have invested substantial time and emotional energy. Although unpleasant, learning that you are not compatible in the first three months is preferable to realizing it after three years, which is often further complicated when children, mutual pets, and shared property are involved.

If you discover that your potential partner is missing a non-negotiable "must-have" trait or is in a "must not have/can't stand" situation, no one is served by continuing the exploration. You must be immediately willing to walk away. Otherwise, you will surely be walking away later in life, and both parties will have paid a dear price for an expensive lesson in love and communication - or lack thereof! You don't want to waste time forcing a fit doomed from the start.

As we noted earlier, it doesn't matter how cute, how sexy, how wonderful this person is in every *other* category, or even how perfect that person might be *for someone else*; when you are in the process of searching for your perfect partner, you *must* honor your top critical screening criteria. These criteria are, by definition, *non-negotiable*, hopefully even with yourself. No wavering here – you are too important!

On-Line Tips

If you brave online dating, be prepared to try multiple services to choose the right relationship-matching program for your needs. E-Harmony is considered one of the best for long-term committed relationships (with an eye towards marriage) due to its careful vetting process. It also has an embedded system[7] created by Dr. Neil Clark Warren, the founder of E-Harmony, based on matching values and criteria such as income and education. Match.com is also suitable for long-term relationships for mature people looking to explore serious and healthy relationships. Of course, there are many adult sites primarily geared towards fulfilling more casual and sexual needs; these are not generally the place to go to for beginning a serious relationship. They can be very desirable sites, however, if sex is your main interest or if casual relationships are what you are most interested in exploring at this time, or even if you are just interested in "practicing" the dating game.

When posting a profile on an online dating platform, you have the opportunity, and in our view, the responsibility, to present an honest and accurate picture of yourself. Be sure to take the time to get current photographs that look like you at your best and most authentic self. We recommend that you have someone review your photos before posting. Our friend found some shots so carelessly done as to be utterly laughable. He considered publishing a humorous coffee-table book containing only pictures from online dating services. (If it were possible to get around privacy concerns, he probably would have done it.) It seems like it should not have to be mentioned,

---

7   Falling in Love for All the Right Reasons: How to Find Your Soul Mate
by Dr. Neil Clark Warren

but from our friend's experience and ours, please double-check your photos. Obvious photo mistakes to avoid include poor resolution, tiny photos, frowning photos; cell phone selfies in the car; all close-ups or all full-length poses; more than one hunting, fishing, football jersey, or beer photo, overly suggestive images, and pictures that include you posed with a different love interest (or looking like you cut that person out of the photo)!

There's a reason for the saying, "A picture is worth those words." When it comes to your online profile, we can't overstate the importance of a good photograph and the thousand words you are communicating. The best way to use the photo section is to include photos that show the range of who you are and what you enjoy doing. Many people say they like exercise and travel or are hopeless romantics. But having a picture of yourself on a bike, in Italy, or taking a shot of a romantic situation and inviting your future partner to join you is much more evidence that you are what you say you are than just your words. No matter what aspects of your life are most meaningful, well-chosen images that place you in the context of what you love will not only say more about you but also attract people with similar interests and provide a starting point for conversation.

Take some time to spruce up your written profile as well. Put some thought into it, and once again, get another opinion from someone who knows you well before you post. Is it poorly written, with careless misspellings? That is easy enough to fix. (Spell check, please!) Is it honest? Does it accurately portray you and what you seek? Is it rambling? Or apologetic? Have you conveyed at least your top three non-negotiables? Try to think of this, not as an advertising piece designed to "sell" yourself. It's not as if you need hundreds of buyers. You want a narrow playing field. Offer enough honest disclosure so that someone who does not fit your needs will self-select out of the pool—and the few who match well readily recognize that you might be a good fit for them.

True Confession

Just because we are considered experts in this field does not mean we are perfect at this process. Dr. Fox thought you might appreciate hearing how she admittedly has not had great luck with online dating. Sifting through disingenuous posts and scams can get wearisome. Browsing through postings, she could not help but roll her eyes at shiny and weather-worn motorcycles and bare-chested men (not her thing). However, the numbers game outside of online dating was not working for her, as she was very involved with work and did not find herself in many social situations to meet new people. A dear friend who had better experience encouraged her to give it one more try. She agreed but insisted on what she saw as a brutally honest profile. Here are some excerpts:

> "… I am pretty content being single and appreciating the advantages. I have always been self-sufficient… But just because I *can* ["do it all"] doesn't mean I always *want* to. There are days when I would love to rely on someone else to drive me to the airport. Or take out the trash. Or massage my feet after a long day.
>
> I miss intimacy most of all. Someone who can carry on an intelligent conversation —and make me laugh; somebody who also reads books and doesn't mind talking about them…
>
> But… it will take a lot to get me out of my comfort zone and into a serious relationship again. That relationship would have to make my life better than it already is (and vice versa, of course). And—I'm a hopeless romantic—there would have to be chemistry. Right away. In my experience, if it is not there immediately, it never arrives. (This may not be others' experience, but it is mine.) I am not getting any younger. I have important work to do in the world, and much as I would love to have a companion along for the ride, I don't have time to wait around for "love to blossom slowly." It would be my strong preference that my partner has a life and ambitions of his own as well.

You need to know that I am complicated, unusual, and busy. I may appear conservative on the outside (though less so as time passes). I spent a lifetime perfecting that facade to please and protect my family, who could not understand me as a child or an adult. On the inside, I think *way* outside the box. I am a "bleeding heart liberal," an original and imaginative thinker, probably an "old soul," highly intuitive and deeply spiritual, and my bucket list includes wanting to travel to the Galapagos Islands, ...and to write and publish several books. I am impressed if you are still interested after reading all of this! And in that case, you might be able to persuade me to spare a few minutes to chat over a glass of wine. Hit "send."

Within twenty-four hours, to her surprise, she received a brief but charming message from a cute but somewhat comic-looking fellow with the tagline (not kidding), "Shirt-on, No Harley." She laughed out loud. How could she resist?

Not one to waste time, she took him up on an invitation to meet for a drink during a rare window of opportunity. She drove directly from work—uncharacteristically, just as she was, without building in time to "freshen up" or perseverate over wardrobe and makeup. Steve greeted her with a winning smile and a hug—immediate chemistry (wink)—and thus ensued one of her life's most breath-taking love relationships. (In the meantime, she received very few additional responses to her post and responded to none of them. She didn't need to.)

Dr. Fox was swept off her feet, and the powerful experience overrode careful consideration of her non-negotiables. Retrospectively, she failed to honor her road map by overlooking one or two red flags (primarily concerning the extended family's willingness to include a new woman in their beloved's life). Instead, she opted to leap empty-handed into the void. Moreover, her story did not have a fairytale ending. I have no regrets - it was a richly rewarding relationship, a well-timed opportunity for learning and spiritual growth. So close, but not quite there, it was time to get back to "sapping" her way back to find her perfect partner.

Consider Using a Personal Guide

Note from Dr. T.: In the middle of a troubling situation, I reached out to a friend for some advice. I shared my distress over a personal issue that was still not resolved after several weeks. After sharing my dilemma, she asked, "Uhhhm, Tina, didn't you write a book on this?!?" "Well, yes," I told her, "But I'm in the middle of this situation. You do realize if I'm in a room with other people, then I'm the only person who can't see my own nose, right?!?" That's when I saw the value of having an objective third-party viewpoint and realized why, as long as humans are human, I would have job security as a therapist! So, if you are having difficulty with any of the material in this book or feeling confused or lost in the middle of your life, consider reaching out to a friend or family member. If you find that difficult to do or simply not helpful, consider contacting a therapist or life coach trained to offer an alternate perspective.

If you feel stuck, a trusted guide may be just what you need to help you see through unconscious drives and overwhelming emotions as you navigate the complex terrain of your journey. A therapist or life coach can help you gain clarity and align your choices with your values. By offering encouragement, feedback, and sometimes "homework," your coach can help you become aware of self-sabotaging patterns in your life and then teach you how to reprogram them.

STEP FIVE:
Confirming Your Choice - Real Gold or Fool's Gold?

Holding the Line Before Going All In

The most important strategy to ensure that you have made a wise choice is to give yourself time without getting overly entangled. And nothing quite says entanglement like becoming sexually involved. Dr. Thomas jokes that once you start being sexual, your opportunity to break up by text is no longer an option! But seriously, moving into a sexual relationship before giving the relationship and your potential partner a little chance to evolve and not taking the time to do due diligence can be costly. Holding back on jumping into a sexual relationship a little later than sooner has some nice benefits. First, you will never be able to get that delicious pre-sexual "courting" stage back once you have crossed the physical intimacy line. If you learn to stretch out the courting phase, you can learn to savor and enjoy the building tension, the flirting, the uncertainty, the butterflies when your potential partner calls, etc. It also gives you time to become friends (which can be a nice perk if you decide romance might not be in your future, but a movie buddy would be nice.) Finally, and most importantly, we have found that it typically takes about 2 to 3 months for some of the underlying patterns and habits that usually don't have time to surface if you only allow weeks instead of months for your assessment period to unfold.

So… we highly suggest you guard against falling into physical intimacy until you are sure you have your basic identified non-negotiable requirements met. It is critically important that when you are with a potential mate, you repeatedly remind yourself about Premise #4: You can stop yourself from falling in love – but once you start – Look out!

Have you ever heard somebody say (or sing): "I fooled around and fell in love"? We don't want to see you slide down that slippery slope before you're ready to fall "all in," so…we have a snippet of advice that we think could be a saving grace. Ready? Okay! No fooling around for at least a week longer than you think is a good idea. (Come on, just give it a try.) Neither of us is by any stretch of the imagination sexually conservative, but…both of us have observed in ourselves and others that jumping into bed before knowing whether your potential partner meets your minimal non-negotiable criteria is risking a lot of time energy and increasing the odds that you might tip the "in-love" scales in favor of spilling those PEA in-love chemicals into your brain prematurely.

> **Remember:** You must have enough personal power to walk away if your partner cannot give you what you require.

Reserve a place for your heart's desire. If you "settle," even temporarily, and fill your available space with less than what you truly want, you do yourself *and* your "less-than-perfect-for-you" partner a disservice. The "temporary" partner will take up space in your world and your heart, and when Mr. or Ms. Right does come along, if you notice them at all, you may not be able or even willing to let them in.

Dodged a Bullet.

They met in a coffee shop. Before a word was spoken, a spark and recognition of mutual chemistry struck them. Some sense of "special something" began to flicker, and their hearts quickened. Mary was on her way out of the coffee shop, and, almost as an afterthought, she gave him her phone number. By afternoon, they were texting, and their exchanges quickly grew into playful flirting. They planned a date.

That first date was just "perfect". They sat at a waterfront restaurant, enthralled with each other. Sam was handsome, intuitive, and successful. Mary was attractive and engaging. almost sparkling; clearly a lover of life. The one-hour lunch turned into a five-hour adventure, ending with a sweet dance at a coffee shop and an even sweeter and more luscious goodbye kiss with the promise of a future date.

After that first date, both of our potential lovers experienced gentle rushes of PEA (phenylethylamine)[8] accompanied by that beautiful, dizzying rush of feeling associated with infatuation, the first stage of falling in love.

Mary reported that she needed to occasionally remind herself to breathe because she was in a semi-breathless state even when she wasn't thinking of him. Sam was already becoming her "mental screensaver"—that is, when she did not have to actively problem-solve or think about a particular

---

8   For more information on PEA, see http://www.asdn.net/asdn/chemistry/chemistry_of_love.shtml.

issue at hand, her mind would drift to thoughts of that best first date ever, the date set for the following week, or vague images of what a potential future might be.

Luckily, Mary did not call everyone she knew and announce that she was falling in love because she recognized that this was only the prodromal period (the beginning "priming" but not the full force state), also known as infatuation. As promising as it appeared, she called her HTFYPP ("How to Find Your Perfect Partner") counselor, who was familiar with the biological basis of in-loveness and the need to proceed cautiously before letting oneself completely fall in love.

At the advice of her HTFYPP counselor, and because of the accelerated quickening of feelings on both sides, Mary asked Sam if he would like her to e-mail her list of non-negotiable desires for a potential mate. He agreed, and the night before their breakfast date, she hit the send button.

The following day, they had a delightful breakfast. They returned to his home for what she thought might be an intimate sharing of even more depth-related topics, such as *his* non-negotiables, his vision for an intimate relationship, and so on. However, when they reached his home while serving her tea, he informed her that even though he thought she was a lovely lady, he did not believe the relationship had the potential to move forward romantically.

Was she surprised? Of course, nearly shocked!

Was she disappointed? Absolutely, almost heartbroken!

Did she know or at least accept that this was the best possible outcome for this relationship? Yes, most certainly, without a doubt.

Later, she discovered that he had made some inaccurate misinterpretations based on her non-negotiable list and jumped to some unfair, and, in her opinion, harsh conclusions about her. Despite her disappointment, she realized that ultimately, she did not want a partner who jumped to conclusions and judgments without verifying his assumptions. Because she had learned to assess her potential partner's mental, emotional, spiritual, and physical maps before surrendering completely, she was relieved that she had not followed her body's wishes to become physically involved before knowing whether they were a match.

The woman's HTFYPP counselor did a debriefing session with her and congratulated her for staying true to her process. The counselor also reminded her that the intensity of the interaction "primed" her to meet "Mr. Possible" and to be careful of the physiological state the two had spontaneously sparked in each other.

Six months later, she found Mr. Right (for her for now) and was grateful that she had dodged the bullet of having to recover from jumping in too soon with Sam!

CHAPTER FOUR:

Quick Review: Avoiding Pitfalls

The Top Five Self-Sabotaging Dangers

All right, you are almost ready. Let's do a quick review of what we think are the top five dangers that can sabotage your chances of getting the perfect partner for you for now:

1. **Not having screening criteria, such as a written map**

   (Be sure to create your list of non-negotiables, which are listed in Appendix B).

When almost anybody shares intimate time with almost anybody else (as in intimate email exchanges, personal stories shared under the influence of alcohol, crises, etc.), a higher than not probability exists that feelings of in-loveness can be created.

Take the example of Bart,–a thirty-something man who follows a healthy lifestyle lifts weights, and participates in triathlons and occasional marathons. While on a business trip, Bart had dinner in a hotel restaurant near a lounge where he met Katie, whom he described as a "drop-dead gorgeous twenty-year-old with a knockout body." He had had a cocktail with his colleagues to celebrate his success that day, and Katie had already had a few drinks celebrating being off work for the weekend. As "fate" would have it, she was "accidentally" seated at his table for one, and Bart, feeling lucky, invited her to stay for dinner. According to Bart, the next hour was "magical." They shared so much in common, the conversation flowed with more wine, and they began to feel like they had known each other forever; and…well…it was the beginning of a crazy, all-out love affair.

But they do not live happily ever after. Within a few weeks, Bart noticed red flags in her behavior, such as not showing up for dates and "forgetting to call" to let him know she would not be there. Then, there were the late-night calls during which her speech was slurred, and her conversations didn't always make sense. Oh, and during one of those conversations, he discovered that Katie was married! She was allegedly in the process of getting divorced (which she was never able to do because of financial concerns and fears of negatively impacting her children). In a few more weeks, he learned that her "knock-out body" was enabled by an eating disorder, and to make matters worse, he learned that she was also a struggling alcoholic. When Katie described her marriage, husband, and work situation, she was always the victim. Later, Bart learned that she was diagnosed with bipolar disorder and refused to take the medication recommended by her psychiatrist. To top it all off, she also appeared to be a pathological liar!

Typically, Bart would have warned his friends about getting involved with such a "challenging package," but the chemical wheels of "in-loveness" had already begun to turn. Under the influence of the love chemicals, Bart fell hard for Katie, who would not have made it through the first 24 hours of his screening criteria if he had taken the time to formalize them.

Unfortunately, Bart spent the next eighteen months in a tangled web. At the end of the "relationship," Bart, a Harvard business school graduate and certifiable "health nut," states that he "barely got out alive" and that after the first week, every day played out like a Jerry Springer episode. After a month of being in the middle of this crazy relationship, someone suggested that Bart try the system described in this handbook. He was shocked to find that this *new* "love of his life" had not one but *four* zeros in his top ten criteria. Four non-negotiable non-starters. So, what was he to do? I'm sorry to say that poor Bart slipped into the second dangerous trap, and that is:

2. **Not honoring your list.**

There is little point in creating your non-negotiable list if you do not honor it. We advise you to put great care and thought into making your list and discerning your non-negotiables *before* you find yourself in a compelling situation with a potential partner that pushes you over the point of no return. The list is the map that provides an anchor, a life raft, and the voice of reason—*your* reason from your deep awareness of what you need and desire.

We can promise that any non-negotiable you let slide by (because everything else was what you wanted) will come back to haunt you and become the issue that can destroy your relationship.

Moreover, take heed: If you change, add to, or remove some non-negotiables *after* you meet someone to justify a less-than-ideal choice, you lose your right to complain (at least to us, that is!)

Bart grew up in an extremely religious family, and in his experience, civic extremism created what he called religious trauma. He remembered shaking violently and throwing up at 11 years old while attending a youth rally because he wasn't "saved." He feared going to sleep at night in case there was a sin that he had committed that he wasn't aware of, and if he died in his sleep before repenting, he might not see his parents in heaven. As a result of the trauma of growing up in a fear-based religion, he often stated that he would never get involved with someone who was uber-religious. You might imagine how disappointing he was to discover that he and Katie did not meet on Sundays because she was attending church (with her family) and belonged to a prayer group that met once weekly to pray and say novenas! (which, to many not-so-religious people, is an indicator of a devout, religious person) When one of his friends questioned his commitment to not being involved with someone highly religious, Bart replied, "Oh, I've been thinking that I need to revisit my relationship with religion." His friend responded, "So Bart, you're already in love, aren't you?" To which Bart could only say, "Uhhhm yes, I guess so." A couple of weeks later, when Bart showed up to a casual dinner date wearing a T-shirt with a picture of the Buddha, Katie became quite upset. Even though Bart was not a Buddhist, just wearing the shirt made Katie feel threatened. They spent many hours having conversations that escalated into arguments when she scolded him for his lack of spiritual growth and disregard for valuing the importance of being "saved." Sigh...

So, there you have it. It happens so frequently that if you are a betting person, you could safely put a couple of hundred bucks on the idea that whatever nonnegotiable item is not honored in the selection process will become one of the issues that will undermine the relationship.

Just ask Bart!

3. Over-riding your understanding to the point of "over-standing."

Here is how this works: We all want to like the person we are falling in love with, so initially, when little human shortcomings present themselves, the very nature of "in-loveness" causes us to minimize them, sometimes to the point of even thinking they are charming, quirky and precious little faults of our beloved.

Let's get back to Bart, who was a very understanding fellow. He understood that his beloved was in a stressful situation. He understood she had some chemical challenges and was trying hard to make her life work. He understood how invested she was in her children and how difficult it was to be married to an overbearing and controlling husband. He understood how alcohol was probably her way of self-medicating. He understood that he needed to be patient because choosing to follow through with a divorce was a difficult process. But he had become *so* knowledgeable that he passed the point of healthy understanding into a pattern of unhealthy "*over*-standing." He understood so much—and excused her behavior so much—that he lost sight of his own needs in the relationship. "Over-standing" can trap a person in an unsatisfying, unhealthy, and even dangerous relationship.

To rectify the situation, Bart would need to come to terms with the truth—the truth, for him, was that no matter how much he understood all the reasons his beloved was not a good match for him, understanding had led to over-standing. He was not getting what he needed to feel loved and happy.

I would like to say that Bart ended the relationship, took some time to regroup, and returned to a healthy pre-relationship state, after which he created his top 10 criteria, followed our recommended protocol, and found the perfect partner. But no, Bart succumbed to the fourth danger, which is:

4. **Getting involved with someone when you are vulnerable.**

It takes a certain amount of personal strength, balance, and self-aware-ness to manage a perfect partner search successfully. We can be especially vulnerable and recovering from a loss of confidence and self-esteem after a personal crisis or loss, especially the end of a profound romantic relationship. Those are the periods of time when to prevent lapses in good judgment, we need to pull back from the playing field, take care of personal needs, and bolster adequate resources. Feeling less than optimal about ourselves can lead to less than optimal (sometimes des-perate) choices.

About three months before meeting Katie, Bart had just ended a relation-ship with a woman who had not been faithful to him (Do we see a theme here?) As a result of feeling betrayed by his wife and best friend, he began to doubt his ability to trust himself. To make matters worse, his business partner was recovering from a mild stroke, so Bart had more work than usual to deal with while his partner was in physical therapy. Often tired and overwhelmed, even workouts didn't give Bart the same boost that he was used to, and more than that, he just missed having someone to come home to and have dinner with. Katie's beauty and youth were healing balm for his injured ego, and sex, at least in the first few weeks, gave him that great "workout" kind of "high," not to mention the burst of PEA's now swirling around in his brain! (Uh-oh…can you say "train wreck"?)

5. **Accepting someone who "has potential" but does not yet meet your criteria.**

Who has felt drawn to someone clearly "below par" compared to our top 10 non-negotiables but in whom we see enormous "potential"? Have you ever found yourself thinking (or saying), "He's going through a rough patch financially now, but he has such enormous earning potential if only he had a little more confidence," or "She could learn to love someone like me if she weren't so distracted by her children and saw how over-involved she is with them." Experience has taught us that the potential to meet any criteria on your list is a poor substitute for meeting those criteria.

Nevertheless, many of us make the mistake of "bending the rules" and loosening up our non-negotiable criteria because we convince ourselves that it is only a matter of time before that potential we see is realized. Sometimes, we convince ourselves (or we are told directly) that we may be the key to that realization, that either by direct effort or osmosis (the influence of our love or glowing personality), we can "fix" someone else. And help them realize their potential. This may be an honorable intention, but it rarely ends well. The potential we see may be real enough, but the fact that we see it says more about *our hopes* for the other person than it says about who and what that person in front of us is now. Please note: Falling in love with potential is never a good idea. Just ask Bart. 10 years later, Katie is still married to the same "loser" husband and has lost her "glow." Instead, she looks withered and harried and never lived up to the potential that Bart hoped she could one day become.

Final thoughts...

So, there you have it. We have outlined the 'do's and don'ts and given you step-by-step instructions for how to find your perfect partner. Our parting last words of advice are: Don't give up! The number one reason this system doesn't work seems to be giving up before your goal is achieved. Think of it like ordering a delicious meal and walking out of the restaurant before your order arrives. The meal is on its way, but you will miss out if you are no longer present.

A Tale of Two Clients

Martha and Mary both started the HTFYPP program within a week of each other. At the nine-month mark, neither had found what they were looking for. Martha was discouraged after her most recent fiasco of a potential relationship start. "I knew it!"

she cried, "this will never work. Maybe it works for some, but not for me."

We never saw her again.

In that same week, Mary came in, also discouraged and crying. "I am so sad. I thought for sure this guy was everything I was looking for, but after last night, I know we are not a good fit for each other." We reminded her that this was the closest one yet and that if she looked at sequential approximations, it reflected a trend: she was getting closer and closer to her desired partner. "I hope so," she replied, "I have come to see through this process how valuable I am and how much I have to offer in a relationship, and I refuse to settle. I am as committed to this process as I am to myself!" She dried her eyes, and as she walked out of the office, she announced bravely, "I got this. It's just a matter of time!".

Eighteen months later, she was crying again,

but this time...

you guessed it... at her wedding!

Hmmmm...

When it comes to love, it's easy to understand that people get disappointed and discouraged when their dates don't meet their expectations, and they do not see evidence that true love is coming. They give up out of disappointment or fear of disappointment, never knowing what they missed. The key to this program is that once you are clear about your desire, you must commit to it for as long as it takes to manifest in your life. (Keep that RAS in gear!) We live in an obliging universe where we can experience all our persistent dreams and desires. One of the biggest obstacles in manifesting what we desire is doubt. Don't give in to doubt. *It may actually be the doubt itself that keeps the prize from arriving.* Knowing opens the door for manifestation. Doubt closes that same door. When you are in alignment with attracting your perfect partner, you must nurture that sense of knowing that they are on their way.

And when they arrive…drop us a line.

We would love to hear about your journey and success!

Cheers, and safe travels!

Perfect Partner Vision Board

First, do some brainstorming. Use images, words, and phrases to explore your relationship needs and desires. You might also think of creating a "vision board"—a large collage on a poster board or foam core board. You may want to hang this somewhere in your home for inspiration.

APPENDIX B:

Non-negotiable List

*Next, write down 10-30 **non-negotiable** traits/qualities/situations*
related to an ideal partner.

1		
2		
3		
4		
5		
6		
7		
8		
9		
10		
11		
12		
13		
14		
15		
16		
17		

18		
19		
20		
21		
22		
23		
24		
25		
26		
27		
28		
29		
30		

Appendix C: Bonus Points

In the table below, write down a few additional traits/qualities and situations that appeal to you and, therefore, might earn "bonus points." –These are not necessarily must-haves or deal-breakers but valuable to be aware of and may become non-negotiables over time.

1		
2		
3		
4		
5		
6		
7		
8		
9		
10		

APPENDIX C:

Dr T's Perfect Partner Non-Negotiables List

Agreement with myself - My future partner needs to BE or DO these things when I meet him and NOT just have the potential to be or do the following. TMThomas

Non-negotiables:

1. Radically honest in a KIND and loving way

2. Has INTEGRITY - does what he says he's going to do

3. Communicates well (thoughts and feelings)

4. HEALTHY - Enjoys exercise and healthy eating

5. Great at Dynamic and JOYFUL Co-Manifesting

6. No history of addiction or has ten years of sobriety (Includes: alcohol, drugs, gambling, porn, etc.)

7. MATURE –

   has personal power; can delay gratification

   balanced and healthy emotionally, mentally and physically

   introspective and self-aware / takes responsibility for action - no excuses

   appreciates and prefers mature women

is a kind king and is happy to have a woman who adores him

8.   SMART - life and relationship smart (way more important than book smart)

9.   9Loves to DANCE (or willing to learn)

10. Good sense of HUMOR – laughs freely

11. ROMANTIC – adores me and treats me like a queen/goddess/ brings me coffee in bed at least half the time / does special things for my birthday/ affectionate/ thinks I'm beautiful – even in the morning!

12. OPEN to new possibilities (costuming, spontaneous trips, personal growth, etc.)

13. Good relationship w mother and former partners and children

14. Children are over seventeen years old. and self-sufficient

15. Normal weight (a few extra pounds okay)

16. Supports me in my speaking career/life's work

17. Non-smoker and non or social drinker (occasional pipes and cigars okay)

18. Capable in social circumstances

19. Sexually compatible (similar appetite and good chemistry)

20. Likes to SNUGGLE and is a good "fit."

21. Supportive of others and SECURE with my healthy and nourishing relationships

22. Prefers to DO something - is a participator more than a spectator

23. Willing to live in Abita some of the time (if I stay here) but able to live anywhere

24. Open to the possibility of living in Florida, Italy, NYC, and Tanzania occasionally

25. Open to playing badminton /pickleball with me and supportive of my fitness goals

26. Has a clear sense of purpose.

27. Travels well and enjoys it

28. Has ample resources (time, energy, and money) and is as generous as I am

29. Emotionally Available

30. Likes my (well-trained) dog

Bonus points for:

1. Intimate social orientation – ideal matching: Intimate /Social/ Self-preservation

2. Able to beat me at badminton (eventually)

3. Likes to cook (and if not, at least likes to cook together)

4. Into Psychology and Personality

5. Knows how to ride a tractor and use a chainsaw

6. Likes plants and gardening

7. Likes couples' yoga / tantric yoga

8. Likes to read and research with me

9. Sensuous

10. Attractive (- engaging smile - soulful eyes)

11. Steady moderate to high energy

12. Likes camping and roughing it - and appreciates fine dining and experiences

13. My family likes him, and he likes my family

14. Flexible time to travel with me

15. Willing to do couple journal every day

16. Can teach me things I don't know and am interested in

17. Likes to give me long foot massages while hanging out

18. Spiritual but not uber-religious

19. Knows how to Tango/Blues and Cajun dancing or willing to learn

20. Willing to learn Italian with me

APPENDIX D:

Review: What Kind of a Relationship

Re-state, in a narrative, the sort of relationship you desire.

Are you seeking someone with whom you want to engage in casual dating, marriage, a hangout partner, or an intimate, long-term relationship?

Use your language to specify your desire.

This could form the basis of your online profile.

The sort of relationship I am seeking:

| |
| |
| |
| |
| |
| |
| |
| |
| |
| |
| |

APPENDIX E:

Note to Future Perfect for You Partner

Finally, write a brief note from your perfect partner (who you will meet hopefully in the near future) thanking you for all of your efforts that have finally led the two of you to be together.

Thank you message from your future partner:

| |
| |
| |
| |
| |
| |
| |
| |
| |

Dr. Tina Thomas, "professional fairy godmother," uses Science and Psychology to help others make their dreams come true. Formerly the clinical director of Tulane's Cancer Counseling Center and research professor at Duke, she is a TEDx speaker and the director of The Gestalt Institute and Relationship Center of New Orleans. She is an RN and LCSW and holds a PhD in Biopsychology. She is also the author of The Ultimate Edge: How to Be, Do and Get Anything You Want (2014) and Who Do You Think You Are?: Understanding Your Personality From the Inside Out (2016)

Dr. Haley Fox is an integrally informed psychotherapist, clinical supervisor, author, and speaker. She holds a Ph.D. in Clinical Psychology, is board-certified in art therapy (ATR-BCCS) and music therapy (MT-BC) and has certification in psychedelic-assisted therapy. Her theoretical orientation is grounded in archetypal psychology, including the role of images in human experience. Her previous writings include Minstrels of Soul: Intermodal Expressive Therapy (2005), Follow Your Bliss: A Soul-Centered Guide to Career-Life Planning (2020), and Sexual Healing: Shining a Lantern on Erotic Experience (2022).